The Daughter's Almanac

Katharine Whitcomb

Also by Katharine Whitcomb

Hosannas
Saints of South Dakota and Other Poems
Lamp of Letters
The Art Courage Program

The Daughter's Almanac

—Poems—

Katharine Whitcomb

....

2014 Backwaters Prize Winner
Patricia Smith, Judge

The Backwaters Press

The Backwaters Press
3502 N 52nd Street
Omaha, NE 68104-3506
(402) 451-4052

The Backwaters Press

thebackwaterspress.org

Published 2015 by The Backwaters Press

Library of Congress Control Number:
2015943343

Cover design, interior design, and typesetting by Éireann Lorsung, ohbara.com

Cover image adapted from *The mystic test book; or, The magic of the cards. Giving the mystic meaning of these wonderful and ancient emblems in their relationship to the heavenly bodies, under all conditions; with rules and processes for reading or delineating the emblems* (Olney H. Richmond, 1919), contributed to the Internet Archive and digitized by the Library of Congress.

The text of this book is set in Cardo, Cardo Italic, and Garamond.

First Edition

Printed in the United States of America
This book is printed on recycled, acid-free paper.

In memory of my mother,
Helga Neuse Whitcomb, 1934-2008

"Time to plant tears, says the almanac."
                                                   —Elizabeth Bishop, "Sestina"

Contents

I. Summer, Posthumous

II. Claret and Gold

III. Winter

Sea Journals: A Sequence

IV. Greening

The Daughter's Almanac

Katharine Whitcomb

I. Summer, Posthumous

Ghost

by the filing cabinet in my small office
I try to eat cold soup, soft summer
dusk at the window & I feel *her*

not some rush of air or howl, no crashing staplers
no translucent floating ghost hovering
near the ceiling the way they do in movies

but as I gather my stack of folders and books
she flickers like thoughts she rests right by my eyes
warm as rose fragrance when you brush a flower

warm as her head stayed for so long after she died
that I waited on the blankets for her to wake up
my hands fluttering to her hair & away again

the warmth there streamed in charged, swift,
near as my vain hope then & now—
not breathing yet not departed, not apart

Summer, Posthumous

Noise seeps through the window—mumbling
cars, goats in the next field chuffing their dried weeds.

Inside, the house cradles many sleeping animals
but no room is dark. You would not sleep late.

You would mow a swath through
my to-do list. You would nail it flat; checkmate!

Me, I moon around in my new glasses. I make peach jam.
I watch British mysteries in the middle of the day.

Jim says, what would she think of you honoring her memory like that?

I say you would think it was neat for five seconds and remind me
I will get into big trouble. Then I put on shoes and run on the windy roads.

Of rivers, I love the small, bright-aqua ones,
fed with streams from the mountains.

You were so sharp and quick.
Of birds, the fiercest.

I despair of honoring you.

I wear your diamonds every day though it is over it is over
and the future falls like a falcon on her prize.

All Night

all night I'm awake while the town falls over
& the cat shatters walls with the power of his love

tree branches spill paper through the open roof
thousands of words rain down while I try to sleep

tree branches rustle their news to my mother
the rosebush newly planted in the earth

tree branches whisper that they will guard me
from harm but the cat says no they won't

the cat says you need a big dog with eyes like Cerberus
you need a big dog to shield us like Athena

my house creaks you need cups of tea & cans of soup
my house sighs you need blankets you get cold

all night I'm awake while the creek sings her song
all evening she laughs after the long morning

the cat yawns & curls a Q on the linen
oh orphan he purrs *lay your head down*

Fawn

her color
buff-hazel
and weariness

following
through the forest
curled beside

in the grass
(fear) (remember)
because trembling

hiding
darting
and camouflage

matching
my mother color
I match my mother

like the forest
quiet (follow) (she
guides me)

curious
slip between
branch and branch

bending
toward/around
fear always

(where is she?)
her color my color
(does she see me?) here

Sweet Time

The glioma pushed on my mother's brain as she floated with a smile
in the in-between. I imagine her lying with her friends on a sun-warmed island,
a rushing river, cheek flat on her hand. She can see someone's blowing hair,
a line of scrub trees, reeds. Current roars with stone-rolling strength, late summer
wind beats noise to the left and noise to the right yet down low in the heat
a calm core free of memory rises and everything she brought with her disappears.

The world is a wolf. His hot breath at the keyhole, his terrible threats—let him wait.

When

you got phone calls at 5:30 in the morning
because the checkbook would not balance
and her knitting wasn't working, you thought
maybe the beginning of dementia
or she'd had a small stroke but by August
she was gone. Mother. Brain tumor. Ashes
in the earth. And how brittle winter would be
after that autumn, how very late the spring.
*When sorrows come, they come not single spies
but in battalions.*

Balfour

After my mother died, my father would not row our boat with me
although I needed his help. We shivered out in the great water,

my awful funeral dress stuffed into the too-small hotel wastebasket
back on shore. He perched on the centerboard in his old striped shirt

and watched me struggle. He never spoke though I could hear him thinking
it was strange to be suddenly battling waves in an open vessel—

the roof lifted rudely off. I said that he must try to take a turn with the oars
then lowered myself over the side with a kiss on his cheek. *Goodbye*

my blankets, goodbye oldest friends, goodbye bodies from which my body was born.
I swam away because I could last long enough to get somewhere else.

Hello tooth-rattling, nerve-buzzing winter, winter sea. And I left him
burned (still burning!) with disease, alone, like a dead warrior king.

Curriculum Vitae

Houdini claimed this birthplace. So do I.
My young mother leaned over me like a paper mill at the falls.

My father sang to me so much that I did not fear
my childhood, which flamed with dream life.

The sky towered azure above my smallness
for thousands of days until I moved alone to the city.

A sunlit pine floor, his steps down the sidewalk
at the end of the day. Music and parties, books around us, treasure.

Then, only this. Do not envy me. I heard
my solitude creaking its dripping wheels even while I was loved.

Remember? They dumped barges of flowers into the sea at Cardiff
while the moon hung above South Dakota, enormous as a catastrophe.

My five ghostless houses, three haunted ones left behind.
Houdini escaped even the chain-wound safe at the bottom of the river.

Late afternoons I sometimes lie down, feel the breeze on my face.
Other kitchens clatter with dinner and my door remains dark.

In my dream the bird lands on my wrist. We go back, you understand,
to the singing, but I don't know what happens after that.

II. Claret and Gold

When Traveling in Airplanes I Always Think of God

especially circling a city before landing at night
when the streetlamps spray the invisible avenues with blown golden seeds.

                         I think of God when the police shoot
King Kong on the tiny screen three rows ahead of me.

                         I think of God in the spring because everything
finally breaks open.

   I think of God when I start awake after re-dreaming a crash against the mountain.

And who have I become? A captive watching them kill the beast?

When we were a little higher up illuminated by our wing lights
the clouds looked solid and edible like God's big cake.

         Once upon a time I thought I heard words meant for me.

I believed I could teach people just by living my life but then I got so tired.

Poem with Backdrop of Boar Hunters in Fluorescent Vests,
  Calling out across the Chestnut Forest

In the Montagne Noire you can lose yourself in the woods, cross valley
after valley without a road. You can follow yellow trail markers in good faith
until they eventually disappear, abandon you to a meadow, overgrown vineyard

or tangled blackberry brambles by a crumbling wall. A marker means nothing!
Markers fall and lie covered with leaves; you can miss the one that leads you home.
Today you chance upon an old farm draped with ivy back in the trees.

The dog makes light of the doorways and stone animal stalls—
Another ruined building he seems to say, tongue hanging, *so what?*
Wind blows in with rain but blows out again. Little owls sleep away the day.

A boar who crosses your path may be fleeing hunters—she wastes no time
disappearing into the undergrowth; she must have escaped the shouting men
who park their trucks outside the village on autumn Wednesdays.

You carry no water. The map lies folded in your pants pocket.
The dog circles close; you whisper secrets into his soft ears.
And still you do not expect the world to love you back.

Through the Window

I am lucky,
Despite
What the rich may think.

My soul is new
On the earth.

These wounds are serious.

God once
Bathed me in brilliance
From the corner
Of the living room.

I remember everything.

A blinding light swept
My head.

I spend my life learning
And will never
Be healed.

Vox

Crazy
for heaven, Alice,
aspiring patron saint of South Dakota,

sings
curly purgatory lyrics
into the ear of the somnolent Pope.

Miracles
drift above
his holy pillow. The Pope snores,

deep
in his Polish childhood.
He has never been to

South
Dakota. Her voice thrums
on anyway like a mile-eating motor,

crooning
hymns of late October,
of how she lay next to the dead

deer
on the scrabbled shoulder,
how she lay down with them and they woke

and ran.

The Hanged Man

Would these words
               wrap around my ankle   like a snake?

                         Snake
who might tie me
               upside down to the beautiful tree
   and hold me, hair
               hanging, above
deep water.

               Meaning not so much
stillness
                         but desire to be shriven:
               confessed,
absolved,
   relieved of burden. Empty-

handed,
               swaying. Whole length of blankness

   like youth. We
cannot last long.
                         Comes harm,

comes

         vanishing.

Time-of-waiting,
               will you bless us,

who are so in need of blessing?
                         The world tires,

         forgets us.

The world can drop

us, breath and bones.

Vermont Suite

1.

Dear O: When the night turns bad, I shake a flashlight
across the yard to the doorless garage and smoke,

watch the farm lights toss across the river. I think of you
most out here. November squalls snow down as it did

on you and me on the deck of your stilted house
in Bethel, flakes burning our eyes. At work they smile evilly

and say the worst is yet to come. And, yes, I believe them
because what else is new? A tire salesman scolded me today

for owning a sedan when I've done so many worse things!
If the power goes out, I check the farm across the way;

dark farm means my fuse box is fine. Did you get those postcards
I rubbed from the wet doorjamb, from the car hood, frozen

cattails, traced in the ice-locked birdseed on the picnic table?
I stay up all night remembering my life, every word of it. Love, K.

2.

Who's there?

Mountain face, facing north. A field above a flooded river. A crouched house.

Have you had a quiet guard?

This body tires but tries. It rises and nails a tarp to keep out the rain.

Who is there?

Sometimes I look around a room at all the faces and love each one in my old way. Then, the good minute goes.

Who hath relieved you?

My burdened ghosts return keening.

What, there? Mad for thy love?

Not, though I have found my small hatreds blazing on the slope. One of them flames very bright.

Looks'a not like the King?

The sight of it gladdens me.

Did sometimes march?

You would think.

How now?

I will not speak to it.

Is not this something more than fantasy?

Daily poison. I do not sleep. I wander and bail the window wells.

What think you on't?

The island a fisherman's dog ran upon disappears beneath the river. Birds float
in the fields.

Doth it make the night joint-laborer with the day?

Yes, in the broken shack, in spiraling snow.

What is't that can inform me?

The apple tree alive with singing.

You have me, have you not?

Only when I feed you.

3.

In my heart there was a kind of fighting
that would not let me sleep but all the ghosts
were my very own, circling the room twice,
three times. At dawn the flickers gobble
seed greedily and pay me no mind.

The mountain's back is turned above
shorn cornfields and river. The night-
curtained light stays on, wedded to
the lexicon. I'll keep the narrative
undisclosed because despite the hand

lettering, painful as quill on vellum,
and though I wait by the mouth
of the well with winter coming, some
ripples, only the wind conspires,
only reflections there indicating

great difficulty. Don't worry; the river
won't pull me in. I'm against tragedy.
I would wed the lexicographer,
would wed again. Let us both be visitors
everywhere. I once saw myself a prisoner

in shackles but, yet again, I was wrong.

4.

Stars through the sea of pine boughs
fire up and out like bobbing torches
in practiced hands, like my own dark
invaders stumbling to a brambled shore.

Above the night meadow the whirl-
pooling snow might emphatically erase
some small stubborn thing but no one
comes close enough to witness.

I'm not staying. The gold is down and
buried; winter shakes his wide white sheets.
I twist the spent flame out. I love every-
thing on earth even more in memory.

Dr. Kim started all his lectures with Moe and Joe
at different sides of the universe and afterward
I would spend evenings grateful for the library basement's
hissing steam heat with *The Dancing Wu Li Masters*
propped open in front of me, reading my homework.
Physics for Poets. PHYS 111. Dr. Kim's narratives sounded like
fabulist tales ending with questions and disclaimers.
A cat in a box? Waves and particles? Uncertainty?
Beyond the library Minnesota winter creaked
and snapped tree branches, fields slept
under long sheets of snow. I just wanted to sit up
all night stoned with my friends playing Elvis Costello
records, watching reruns of *The Twilight Zone*
and laughing. To surround myself with energy.
I leaned over my book: *The real problem is that we are used to
looking at the world simply.* This physics defies
conceptualization, impossible to visualize.
A science of the unverifiable. Planck, Born, Heisenberg
theorize toward a mystical vision of unity.
I thought about quantum theory in the studio
while Professor Celender lectured on Duane Hanson;
I thought about consciousness as Dr. Ward discussed
the exploitation of the Victorian underclass.
I was so young then my heart hardly stayed in my body,
always imagining the unimaginable. Of course things change
because we observe them. I could buy that.
I could buy *consciousness* and an endless profusion
of possibilities. Particles annihilate themselves
in beautiful ways. We almost crashed the car
driving home from Octoberfest burning on
windowpane acid, left the gas station without paying
because we forgot. Winter forced us inside those
brick buildings where I sat still enough to read
for a few hours. The big wooden table hummed
under my elbows. I had notes from PHYS 111
about rooms moving through space, baseballs, closed elevators,
Michelson-Morley, Lorentz, time-travel! All those particles
blowing up and making themselves new. Feynman's
diagrams looked like sculptures, like petals, and
in my notebook I had written *Each part of reality
is constructed of all the other parts.* A slice of time, with infinite
parallels, there in that place, vibrating and open-ended.

Tobacco Heart

I dreamed a silhouette hazed in elegance, flare between her lovely fingers. A siren-self, chanteuse. Such a charmer. And who could resist her? In Prague and San Francisco, Wisconsin taverns, living rooms in Alaska—she whispered *Have one. With me.* You and me together and him too. All of us in dragon-smoke, at the kitchen table where I spoke a Sanskrit poem with fire in my hand. She whispered, *Darling.* Sometimes, palpitating and sick, I placed one hand pledging allegiance, the other on my stomach and repeated my name *Katharine* until I feel calmer. And I know this part is over, done to death, all this noise. The gestures and pacing, the coquetry. All those huddles over flame in the wind, brother and sister of it, mingled sex, map made of burning. I reached for contact; brought it into my mouth like religion.

Blasted

sometimes old anger comes back with the third drink drops in-
to open air like a trapdoor in my brain falling free the attic

stairs unbend breath of dust downward *who are you?* any-
one better run fair warning gun cracked back there clinked

ice clicked in the tumbler gears of the lock slip-
ping into place oh person love does not matter now not

here what good is the heart and what is the mind for—
if the slipcover makes a real ghost from its furniture?

The Plan of Ms. Wenz to Marry Up

Dashing Colonel Brandon rides up on a white horse while she is playing
   the pianoforte,
but that only happens in the Jane Austen novels Ms. Wenz reads at Book Club.

Ms. Wenz's hours got cut in June. She checks out *Sense and Sensibility* from the library,
self-conscious that she is there, *sans* toddler in tow, in the middle of the day.

The red house she bought when she first moved to town became a burden;
a blonde realtor pounded the FOR SALE sign into the dirt by the front gate yesterday.

The Austen books have inspired a new plan in Ms. Wenz: A. an apartment is cheaper
B. she can still plant cilantro in pots C. she'll join Anytime Fitness with her extra
   money

and D. lose some weight. There is E. the question of being a thirty-five-year-old
single waitress and the last boyfriend still a bad taste in the back of her throat.

F. G. H. spiral into online dating: her photos, her profile, all that searching through
emails. She draws the line at driving over an hour in a borrowed car for a coffee.

I. is a first date tonight, the prospect of which made her think of J. her wedding
colors: eggshell, white and K. what her something borrowed and blue would be.

Ms. Wenz sits at the Lone Star waiting for Tractorguy, as he calls himself on
   Match.com.
"Trac" looks swarthy and self-sufficient in the snapshots he posted on his match-page.

She hesitates before ordering a pint but then he is late and she needs something to do
with her hands. The printout of Trac's profile soaks up moisture under the glass.

This feels sad like the end of a summer party, she thinks. Like moving beer bottles
back to the fridge from the cooler, like tossing the cake so you won't eat it all yourself.

"'Tis Bitter Cold and I Am Sick at Heart"

my friend telephones to tell me
she is marrying a man she met a month ago

everyone else is shocked but she and he
are calm about it and what can I say to her?

that love is coherence? yes and how
the Ecuadorian woman seated next to me

on the plane explained the perils of caution
and extolled passion

but my heart feels wrapped in mesh

these haunted winter nights vast
as mansions boomerang with memory

a woman walks down the street slowly
guiding a toddler by the hand

and it should not be that I sit too long
at the stop sign to watch them but I do

my friend suggests building a shrine
might help me find somewhere to call home

the purpose of living alone
of flying low to the ground is to gain speed

is to read the fields is to hide
from those who would harm us, yes?

this pounding without bells or ocean
what, is Katharine there? a piece of her

Departed Cordelia

My father said, *You are a spirit. Where did you die?*
and we were equally alive. I thought to correct him
but he was not in his perfect mind.

My answer, to myself: *still, still, far wide,*
wide of the mark, wide of this world and time.
My father said, *You are a spirit. Where did you die?*

and I kissed him as he slept, wild-haired, sliding
down in the chair. My kiss would be his medicine
if he was in his perfect mind.

We met again in prison, he and I. For a while
his memory cleared. I wept that he knew my name,
my father who'd raved, *Spirit, where did you die?*

From the beginning my heart held my words aside
and he sent me with France, to battle, to the storm.
He was not in his perfect mind.

I left forever. I'm dead as earth. I gravely
flowered, a rose in the rain, a dark bowl of flame.
My father said, *You are a spirit. Where did you die?*
but he was not in his perfect mind.

Unbidden

bridge of my chest labors   whenever I relive it
phone clicks quiet battens down batters nothing
                                  bumping into nothing clicks off clicks
                      out
                        shhhh

to think on it rips another dress from the nail
looses long stitches shoulder to shoulder
snags the snarled sleeves   until I can't feel my hands

how then will I circle the seam left
how will I reason the chafe and age left

whenever I relive it   phantom seizes   on each curved rib ridge

this is at least not confused with god this is at least not conformed
                to good this is not at last confirmed
                            by anyone
only lashed breath
                from the cringe of my hips to the cage of my head

a sheet around my legs in an undressed room

whenever I relive it phone snickers *off*   flickers   *out*

how then do I crack the spine of silence
how will I sleep with those peeled miles unspooling hour after hour unmarked

unwed in the heaved blank air

whenever I relive it weight cracks the violet space above my clavicle

to think on it spills the sand from a buckling cliff where the trail curls back on itself
the way smothered over the day blundered over
my wariness snared a bloody bearing   *off* the compass

a floating needle torn *out*

how then will I take another boned blow
another borderless ever after   how will I fold myself

ungloved into the netherworld

whenever I relive it   phantom muzzles his six-eyed dog

    phone winks   phone sinks

this is at least not salvation this is not the next   mud-caked companion
but a burrow lined with torn paper

    a wall scrawled with chalk in the handless black

whenever I relive it

Dream on His Birthday

The rain drums. We run through the house plugging leaks together. And I have not seen him for so long. We broke fast. *I thought changes were holy.* To rush away full of hope is to invite the whip and I was whipped. Am. To leave a faithful heart in all its obeisance, then stumble out to the wind is to be diminished. (NO!) Yes. To pull myself wet up the ladder again. I thought that one so determined, so *brave*, would not be sitting past dinnertime alone five years later weeping over her own desecration. At gunpoint! I want it GONE—pretentious sad stump of a world. As if. I could. Today this dream was proximal and breathed rain; my once-husband unbidden, mine again. If I leave our old house I'm afraid my fingers might unclench his forever. I still have those *clothes*.

This Is Where Things Stand on the Twenty-Seventh of October

Windshields of parked cars fur with frost most mornings. Leaves
sleet off the aspens with the slightest breeze, Pollacking the yard
all claret and gold. Trim is unscraped. A new stair unstained.

No large trash bags anywhere in the garage. The cat sleeps inside
until sun strikes the porch. Mysteriously thawed food lies dumbly
on a freezer shelf. Someone needs to be called to check the furnace,

and fridge; someone should ring the clinic too. The prescription
renewal is conditional. Insurance documents must be faxed
so the refi goes through. No fax without a landline. Files fly out

into the ether. Wet clothes drape the drier. The cat roams fence tops
each afternoon; he patrols the sliding glass door for movement inside.
Hey, I say, *hey Pooter, if you killed anything I don't want to know.*

Against Melancholy

In the fierce old days every word you uttered was remembered forever
and not in a good way—this made you want to move to a very quiet place
by yourself and you did—never guessing the light of your beauty
was merely youth—people you love would die or try to die—
your judgment would falter—and then you were alone but more so,
like thinking France but then finding yourself deep in the forest
having stumbled upon an ivy-covered abandoned stone village
with a boar running by—not just France, but, as they say, *la France Profond.*
Sure—alone, then alone in the middle of your life in the middle of the night—
in a dark wood wandering. In truth, animals and lovers sleep next to you,
under your mother's quilt. You feel her hand on your hair. And after
many times hearing no and another no, there is yes, even if followed by no again.
Still remarkable: chestnut trees. Bicyclists by the water. The kindness of strangers.
In the fierce old days someone wrote you a card that said *I love you completely.*
Someone wrote this and mailed it to you and you did not write back.
He is alive somewhere married to someone else. He is alive with his big heart
and that turns the world for a while—this shimmering and raining-on-itself world.

III. Winter

Sea Journals: A Sequence

Sea Journal

Visited-one, dwelt-in-one, I roll these memories on my tongue the way a soul slides in the sleeping flesh & smoky breath. That is to say, I stagger toward you. That is, in spite of, despite all, affliction, I make my way.   O friend, the landscape rushed streaming fields past the windows as I drove with my legs trembling, blazing all winter in fever dream. Ordinary ceased. No lag now, my terror, but flood. Of what are you? What *of* you?

What left, O-help-me, what is leaving?

                      This tide snows & snows.

Will you fill your arms?
                      Will you lie with me here on the underwater road?

Sea Journal

Code over the water; snow streaked the winkle-scattered sand. Beach flung with
medallions. Code, our hand-to-hand; code, each word a dalliance. Code, *you get me?*
In the cold wind there was no ivory fan, no lamp-lit room, no perfumed dress.
Lover, this account works on the surface, semaphores across a page: my ungainly
traveled laughter. See how much I want everything still. Code, *what I'm implying*. And
how foolish not to offer (say it—*to give*) that which is mine.

Sea Journal

Meanwhile, I shucked my shelter. Meanwhile. Writes Hopkins, *What you look at hard seems to look hard at you hence* . . . will it open? Hard enough will it change like that sky so fused, so soaked one can only, one need only lie down in it? As I did. Blue of swoons, blue bruise, great inkdark, fogdark bank of night. Elephantine blue-sheered night. Lost toppled moon on her back in blue, loose in her bearings, lost in something other than thought, other than mind, than dream. Blue enough to devour. Blue to oblivion.

Sea Journal

Occasion is everything; form follows feeling through the slushy streets; I could be the tired woman with a cold who quits work early and lies down in an empty house, her small upstairs bedroom tight as the stanza she thought she might write and she falls asleep as snow sifts down, hours of it settling over the town like a dream everyone is sharing; I might toss and cough and slide into the motion of harbor light sinking as she does, chest laboring, there where sand and sleet stream sideways across the road, where the land finally does end and all travelers have to stop; I would slip away, a leaf over the ice, away from my own bright youth and youth's leave-taking, sigh stitching sigh all through the bruised night.

Sea Journal

In sleep each chapter of this book turns like a body rolling over. Each page a clean mystery. If somebody asked me to lie next to him and tell him, what would I tell? Nesting doll, locket, little box, would I take it out? Steady fierce dream in a deep suitcase, cursive from a crabbed hand balled inside a cheap coat pocket. Baggage and undercarriage. Dwelling place: sea-tower locked with tremors. A dream of following the beach trail moving over it slowly word by word but I woke fevered and still I was lost.

Sea Journal

Simple *x*. Simple *o*. Schematize the pattern as follows: a bad dream, piano music
washing down the street.   Fragments fall on me.   Door swings open, shut,
in the wind.

Late sun creaks through every gap, blazing
the whitewashed room and the snow glows impossible blue-gray.   Every breath
smells of the sea. Winters he works past dark.

Like a moth I keep living, high-pitched, transparent wings hard on the glass.

Sea Journal

Pain so brilliant how could I but change.

Sea Journal

He writes that weeks go by when no one touches him but I think of the cats
lantern-eyed, kneading his ribs. Day is bone, feather-gray ash. Day barely lights
the sky. Worn down by the weather I leave my epiphanies on the jetty—abandon
the car, sand road, song that led me away. There are worse things than failure or
poverty, wouldn't you say? I have been waiting (day is feather, day is bone) like the
beach pine blown backwards all winter, in a dull dress I've never changed. *To set
one's mind*

  to abandon *to leave* *to wait* *is worse, is far.* O my own grief-wrung
 heart,

       madness maker, be my one compatriot

   now, my conspirator.

Sea Journal

Rain-stark, in the wind. Nights play out roiled and pitched. It was quiet when I woke. Quiet with a small universe of phantoms, pillowcase, long nightclothes. Blacked beat of blood whimpers in my ears. My letters say *Roses still in bloom but the dunes creep closer, the dead drift above their huge vacant lot. The whole day is like night.* Deep. Sea exhales all buffet and tang. It was quiet when I woke. For some things we are sorry forever.

Corners where he once slept turn themselves out like empty pockets.

He was the smoke in the damp fireplace, a terror shaking the dry-needled tree.

He shrugs into his coat, limps stiffly under the lintel,
blue-knuckled hand on the knob.

He was the wind scouring the panes with vodka-cold breath.

Bang the door shut after him!

Throw the bolt!

Let me leave the story there.

IV. Greening

Horse Dream

That my beauty
was a weighty mane,

and a muscle-body heft
with life. My range great

golden fields, changeable. *Gone.*
Beloved, where are you,

one I have waited on these
many men, these many lives?

My falling cliffs,
wide open pasture. Please

forgive this persistence.
You can hear me, kicker

at the threshold, lost mare
sore-shinned from running

over the soaked fields.
Darkness breaks when I turn

my heavy head; water for thirst,
a place out of the wind. Stable

yard or door ajar, lit,
your gauzy silhouette

beckoning. I have chosen
my places wrongly yet I will ask,

I still bow my neck,
that you might touch me.

How Flatterers Must Be Shunned

in May your almond trees flung
armfuls of wild perfume at the moon all night
and we could drink the scent through the kitchen window
screen like stream water, the blossoms' incandescence
hooded until daylight when I would drive home
stunned as someone who's seen a powerful movie
that reminded them of beauty,
pictures replaying as I rolled through the desert
rewinding until I fell asleep in my own bed alone
and dreamed of ribbon-trimmed dresses blowing
on a summer clothesline.

in the beginning you phoned me to discuss God
and I said let's go down that road and don't worry
if it narrows to one lane we'll be fine
but when I thought you might speak you plucked a toothpick
from the ashtray; you turned the radio on.

deer in the yard live almost tame. your dog rested
tethered to a post on grass littered with petals.
the fawns knew her and did not flee. everything
belonged to you. even that honeyed air arcing over us
smelled like your hair after a bath dampening a cotton pillowcase.
how wary and worn out we were back then
when May released your young blooming trees.

The Prince's Almond Trees

The poet has chosen to use third person in this essay to relieve the weight of the "I." The poem's title comes from Chapter XXIII in some translations of *The Prince* by Niccolo Machiavelli. The title has also been translated as "How to Avoid Flatterers." To use this as the title of a poem that explores the erosion of a love affair is intentionally coy.

The speaker of the poem addresses a "you." In the poem, "you" owns almond trees. In bloom. "You" is a dentist the poet met online.

Courts are always full of flatterers.

"You" lives in Idaho still perhaps. The poet does not know for sure. The poem is set in May. The poet tries to remember which year. The poem was written in October after the poet had left "you." In the poem the blossoms glow like candles.

One must employ terrorism or kindness, as the case dictates. "You" employed both.

The poet loved the dentist's dog much more than she loved the dentist. She did not, in fact, ever love the dentist.

"You" courted her first with phone calls about the nature of religion.

Severity is usually more effective, but humanity, in some situations, brings better fruit.

As a child, the poet loved a book illustrated with watercolors by Tasha Tudor. The phone calls were insufferable. She leaned toward them nevertheless.

Reader: if you are a literalist, events in the poem are true.

Religion must be fostered even though it may be false, provided it is a kind that preserves social solidarity and promotes manly virtues.

"You" spoke at length about Buddhism. The poet's favorite illustration depicts a little girl hanging sheets on a clothesline in the wind. The caption beneath reads *warm, beautiful summer.*

"You" is not a Buddhist.

Do what you must do in any case, but try to represent it as a special favor to the people.

The little girl's dress blows behind her and the ties on the dress float upward. "You"'s house is set back off the road between old pastures. Deer love to sleep under his pine trees. The character, Ingrid Fleming, in Louis Malle's film *Damage*, beats herself with a knotted dishtowel when she discovers the truth about her husband.

If you must commit a crime do not advertise it beforehand.

The poet had never seen almond trees before. The phone calls prompted her to visit "you" in Idaho. While writing the poem, she remembered the smell of the trees and the long drive to get there and to get home again. In person "you" was not so talkative. "You" could not think his way out of a box. She remembered *The Prince* and those little watercolors. The poet was loath to dismiss "you" and his startling trees in spite of herself.

This is not a flattering revelation. "You" became the poet's knotted towel for a while.

Reader: if you are a literalist, we are done.

She made those journeys between Washington and Idaho thinking about Machiavelli, Louis Malle, Tasha Tudor, the wheatfields, the desert, and not "you."

Men should either be caressed or annihilated; appeasement and neutralism are always fatal.

"You" understood power. There was only one almond tree. That October she wrote "everything belonged to you" and by then she was long gone.

Poem Ending with a Line by Mick Jagger and Keith Richards

This cowboy town is so small that if you step out onto your front porch your insane colleague is sure to screech around the corner in her old minivan, your star students will skulk past on their way home from a kegger, and your old boyfriend will roll by in his three-quarter-ton pickup with its special Allison transmission kit you heard plenty about. Your old boyfriend is on his way to his new girlfriend's house. The bartender at the only bar in town is your former student and you know the couple at the next table over because for five minutes you went to Rotary lunches and Gold Buckle dances with the old boyfriend in his truck and he knows everyone in town. Everyone in town sends you real estate info and asks how you are with pained expressions on their faces. Sometimes you imagine they are pained because your hair is dirty or you are at the red-faced end of a long run and sometimes you just cannot hold a conversation because the whole previous hour you were crouched on the floor of your tub with a washcloth in your mouth. Sometimes you are in the Super One buying wilted chard after trying to call a friend who is not awake yet in her faraway city. Sometimes the faraway friend is on new medication and she cannot pick up the phone. You walk into the bar and your old boyfriend is with his new girlfriend or he is alone and says something to you about the bookcase he dropped off at Goodwill and how it might be there if you still want it and if this were the old Old West and not the new Old West you would call him out onto Pearl Street. Then the radio ad reps and real estate agents and geography professors would put down their microbrews and come out on the boardwalk to watch. You would call him out for no other reason than he complained your cooking was too healthy. The bullets fly. Bleeding, you send a telegram: He shot me once STOP but I shot him twice.

Love Letters

Travelers in shoreless countries always write love letters
as if they were the first to do so. During the long-syllabled hours
of April and May they write cramped in their tiny *penzions*,

at rain-splotched café tables, on the steps of the cathedral.
They write of swallows screaming like children in the purpling air,
they write from the middle of the continent

that all cities are common in their dailiness. Travelers lean into
the learning of practical rituals—currency, tram stops, aperitifs—
the way a drunk woman leans against a doorframe

to watch the rain, easily, so that soon the motions become habit.
The crowds on the subway part to let them in and no one looks up
when they speak. Old buildings blacken in the haze of history.

Strange groceries relax in their dark shopping bags,
their money flutters to rest in many different pockets. So many
heads have lain here before that these pillows find no mystery

in their particular soft hair. Across the miles every love letter
has wind in it, the travelers have to work hard
to make the words stick. From this distance,

they have to weigh them carefully. Why are they here,
each of them, alone? Why do their bodies frighten them,
so they refuse comfort again and again? The ocean that separates lover

from lover says to be filled you must first make yourself empty,
but the travelers are too deep in the ancient city's heart to hear
anything except the hour sounding across the cobbled square.

The words they write, meant to transfigure the past, come out
gray as confusion, cursive as smoke
in the sun's last rings of light. The fine and terrible

truths of the landlocked float with swans down petal-flecked rivers.

Star

so the day is long and later on an empty bed:
it may be only self-encouragement to even
imagine a clear channel to heaven, where dead ones
dream in breathy ether, but what if the birthed
are lucky, what if that impossible cartoon hand,
large as a gym class trampoline,
does cradle us? what if, inexplicably,
the soul's devotion does lift the roof off and

leave us open; the good work of lace-making
or tightening a girder or joining a dance
is a jar filled with the water we need to live,
where we find stars reflected, real, floating
and may drink it down to remember a cadence
from childhood, giving back all we had to give?

Intercession to the Saint of the Reading Room

Catherine of tanners, saint of turners, of millers and maidens
and nurses, of preachers and potters and scribes,
lift this moment from the page and bend near.

Travel in time to a room where a fourth grader
lies on her trundle bed reading each book
Miss Elrod gives to her. Visit when she hides inside the cloak
of the books, inside Narnia, Earthsea, and Middle Earth,
where the boys with their snowballs can't get her
nor the strangers and old people she must pass,
not even the psychedelic pink shag carpet
that sometimes swirls at night like a nest of ropy snakes.

Saint of archivists, remember who I was.

Catherine of the apocryphal profile, saint of apologists
and spinsters, of libraries and jurists and girls,
Catherine of the suppressed cult, I have been walking through
your meadow with my heart's own flagellant fiction.

Catherine-whisked-up-by-angels, I found a hall therein.

First

This kiss is like a dress falling off a tall building,
no, higher! Floating from the top of the Space Needle.

This kiss is queen-size, XXXL, and cups the air
softly (spring in Seattle!), in no hurry at all.

You could take this kiss to a party and walk it home;
you would introduce this kiss to your really good friends.

And as the kiss leaps away in the middle of sightseeing
you know no other kiss has ever come close. Forsake

all the rest and catch your breath, your racing heart.
This kiss is suicidal, inconsolable, and utterly rare.

Air

Last night wind tore at the vents
startling the cat but now a pink tree
across the street stretches lacy sleeves:
a still life. Calm. I love spring
for gentleness after the back-stiffening
months, after all that living-through.
Finally, at the right time of day, air
is a kiss. Thank you. Dusk's cool hand
strokes the back of the neck but late,
and less and less. I'm ozone-soaked
sky, flashing lightning high up,
disturbances, unsettled atmosphere.
Heat hitting snowmelt. I wish I were
simpler: one glorious flowering, then
steady green for a light-filled season.

Poem without Ferocity

Deep breath before drinking morning coffee.
Outside in the wind, leaves blaze greening sap, lit
fuses. April slides to May more luscious
each day. My lover drives away early
as I sometimes do across town, to the squawking
of crows. We leave each other happy, intent on the day.
I could live inside of April the way the air reverberates
now—frogs singing *wake up*, and I'm already awake.

Animal Heaven

As if diving from a dock the dogs leapt off a railroad bed
today over the sunken hayfield. They plunged
into the wake of grass, gold one, black one, and disappeared,
reappeared in the breaking green troughs, at a run.

Now here we are. Our tall bedroom sways;
frigate ship steered by gravity. Your arms reach to soothe
me when I wake shaken from a nightmare, another long chase
to the horizon—the dogs breathe with calm huffs and woofs.
Soft eyes closed, the Golden's paws move like herons'
wings in the west pasture, undulating muscular bounds.

Through the tall grass heaving with the bosomy wind of June,
sleep lowers us. With garments undone our love eases down
to the valley floor. The dogs swim one before, one
after. All this beauty! In waves, then oblivion.

.

Notes

The last two lines of "When" are from *Hamlet* by William Shakespeare.

"Curriculum Vitae," Lines 1 & 2: Harry Houdini claimed to have been born in Appleton, Wisconsin, like me. In fact, he was born in Budapest, Hungary, but he was anxious to appear more "American" to his public.

"The Hanged Man": The poem refers to the # 13 Major Arcana card in the Tarot deck.

"Vermont Suite": The italicized lines in part 2 are questions asked by the night watchmen in Act I of *Hamlet* by William Shakespeare. The first two lines in part 3 are also quoted from *Hamlet*.

"'Tis Bitter Cold and I Am Sick at Heart": The title and last line are answers to the night watchmen's questions in Act I of *Hamlet*.

"Intercession to the Saint of the Reading Room": This poem is addressed to Saint Catherine of Alexandria, the famous Catherine of "the Wheel."

"First": This poem borrows its first line from Norman Dubie.

Acknowledgments

I gratefully acknowledge the editors who published these poems, sometimes in earlier forms and with other titles, in the following journals:

"Unbidden" in *Alaska Quarterly Review*
"Balfour" in *Bellingham Review*
"Love Letters" in *Crab Orchard Review*
"When Traveling in Airplanes I Always Think of God" and
  "'Tis Bitter Cold and I Am Sick at Heart" in *Floating Bridge Review*
"Curriculum Vitae" in *Mississippi Review*
"Departed Cordelia" in *The Missouri Review*
"The Hanged Man" in *Narrative*
"Tobacco Heart" in *Pontoon 9* and *Encore: More of Parallel Press Poets*
"First" in *Pif: The Arts and Technology Magazine*
"Dream on His Birthday" in *Post Road*
"Sea Journal [code over the water]" and
  "Through the Window" in *Provincetown Arts*
"Sea Journal [meanwhile]" in *Shankpainter*
"Sweet Time" and "This Is Your Brain on Physics" in *Sweet*
"Sea Journal [in sleep each chapter]" and
  "Sea Journal [rain-stark, in the wind]" in *Tertulia Magazine*
"Star" in *Washington English Journal*
"Vox" in *The Yale Review*

"Fawn" and "This Is Where Things Stand on the Twenty-Seventh of October" were published in the *Jack Straw Writers Anthology*, Vol. 15, Jack Straw Productions.

"Poem without Ferocity" was published in *Fire on Her Tongue: An eBook Anthology of Contemporary Women's Poetry*, Annette Spaulding-Convy and Kelli Russell Agodon, eds., Two Sylvias Press.

"How Flatterers Must Be Shunned" and "The Prince's Almond Trees" were published in the anthology *Making Poems: Forty Poems with Commentary by the Poets*, Todd Davis and Erin Murphy, eds., Excelsior Editions, State University of New York Press.

"When Traveling in Airplanes I Always Think of God" was selected for *Verse Daily*, September 1, 2008.

A number of these poems were published in the 2009 Floating Bridge Chapbook Prize Winner, *Lamp of Letters*.

"Balfour" was a finalist for *Bellingham Review*'s 49th Parallel Award for Poetry.

Thanks to Yaddo, the Whiteley Center, and the Fine Arts Work Center in Provincetown for time, space, and support.

Thank you to my friends, my brother and sister writers, who believed in these poems: Mark Wunderlich, Jesse Lee Kercheval, Todd Davis, Xavier Cavazos, Elise Forier Edie, Susan Rich, Derek Sheffield, The BookLifters, and Joe Powell.

Thank you to John and Kerry at La Muse and Kathy and the crew at Whiteley Center.

I am grateful for being part of a wonderful writing group: Elizabeth Austen, Kathleen Flenniken, Peter Pereira, Dianne Aprile, Jared Leising, and Sylvia Pollack. Your support and encouragement mean the world to me.

I owe endless gratitude and love to my father, Richard Whitcomb, for being an example of optimism and intellectual courage.

To the judge, Patricia Smith, and to everyone with The Backwaters Press (Jim Cihlar, Cat Dixon, Greg Kosmicki, Éireann Lorsung)—thank you for honoring my book with your enthusiasm and support.

CPSIA information can be obtained
at www.ICGtesting.com
Printed in the USA
FSOW03n1010170316
18074FS

9 781935 218388